Red Stilts

Also by Ted Kooser from Copper Canyon Press

Kindest Regards: New and Selected Poems

Splitting an Order

Delights & Shadows

Braided Creek: A Conversation in Poetry (with Jim Harrison)

Red Stilts

Poems by
Ted Kooser

Copper Canyon Press
Port Townsend, Washington

Cover art: Don Williams, *Nebraska City Alley,* oil on panel, 11 × 14 in.

Copper Canyon Press is in residence at Fort Worden State Park in Port
Townsend, Washington, under the auspices of Centrum. Centrum is
a gathering place for artists and creative thinkers from around the
world, students of all ages and backgrounds, and audiences seeking
extraordinary cultural enrichment.

LIBRARY OF CONGRESS CATALOGING-IN-PUBLICATION DATA
Names: Kooser, Ted, author.
Title: Red stilts / poems by Ted Kooser.
Description: Port Townsend, Washington : Copper Canyon Press, [2020] |
    Summary: "A collection of new poems by Ted Kooser, former US Poet
    Laureate"— Provided by publisher.
Identifiers: LCCN 2020017231 | ISBN 9781556596094 (cloth) |
Subjects: LCGFT: Poetry.
Classification: LCC PS3561.O6 R43 2020 | DDC 811/.54—dc23
LC record available at https://lccn.loc.gov/2020017231

ISBN 9781556596490 (paperback)

98765432 FIRST PRINTING

COPPER CANYON PRESS
Post Office Box 271
Port Townsend, Washington 98368
www.coppercanyonpress.org

Acknowledgments

Able Muse: "On the Market"

The Briar Cliff Review: "Sixtieth Reunion Banquet"

The Chattahoochee Review: "Suitcase"

Great River Review: "Sounds of a Summer Night"

The High Window (UK)*:* "Apron," "A Caesura," "In Early August," "Recital," "Starling"

The Hopper: "At Dusk, in December"

The Hudson Review: "A Shadow," "Vespers," "Vulture"

Kenyon Review: "Raspberry Patch," "Woolly Caterpillar"

Mantis: "Deer Path"

The Midwest Quarterly: "A Moth, a Moon," "Noon Whistle," "An Overnight Snow," "Rain after Dark," "Spring Landscape," "Up the Block"

Mississippi Review: "A Floating Bottle"

New Letters: "Mother and Child"

Nimrod: "Shame"

North American Review: "A Letter"

Plume Poetry 7: "A Roadside Cemetery"

Poetry East: "The Couple"

Rattle: "A Town Somewhere"

A Ritual to Read Together: "Rabbit Hutches"

River Styx: "House Moving"

Solo Novo: "Red Stilts"

Terrain: "Farmyard Light"

3rd Wednesday: "Fairgrounds," "Ohio Blue Tip"

Viking Dog Press (broadsides)*:* "After a Heavy Snow," "Tree Frog"

Virginia Quarterly Review: "At Dawn"

West Branch: "A Heron"

I am grateful to my wife, Kathleen Rutledge, and to Pat Emile, Steve Hahn, Judith Harris, Katie Schmid Henson, Suzanne Ohlmann, Connie Wanek, and P. Ivan Young for their helpful suggestions. And to the generous supporters of Copper Canyon Press who make these books possible.

For Kathleen

After he'd walked away, she stood in the yard
in starlight listening to dogs bark, each more faintly
as he passed the farms along the road.

"Father Sergius," Tolstoy

Contents

I

II

III

IV

V

Red Stilts

I

A Letter

You couldn't have known of my parents,
who lived in Iowa, where they'd been born
and where they'd worked together in a store
and fallen in love and were married. Father
was thirty-five and Mother twenty-seven,
old to get started but not too old in those
hardship Great Depression nineteen thirties
when people had to wait for everything.

That first year they had an apartment
across from a park where the town band
held its summer concerts, in a band shell
rainbowed with rows of hidden, colored bulbs
that slowly shifted with the music's mood.
Imagine that, young families on blankets
spread on the grass, with their open faces
reflecting cool violets and blues.

You have to imagine all this, as I have,
for I was only a child in those years.
Imagine Dick Day, the town's bandmaster,
in his black-billed cap, black uniform
with yellow piping running down the legs,
the fish-like mouths of the flashing trombones
appearing as if they were trying to catch
the little white tip of his flying baton.

Oh, the noise! That silvery fife coming in
on the minute, the boy with the triangle
waiting and waiting and waiting, then *ping!*
Tubas nodding and burping and honking,
and fanfares of brass, the bandmaster's hanky
snatched from his pants like a referee's flag,
swiped under his cap, then swiftly stuffed back
where it was without dropping a beat.

Imagine, too, this painted popcorn wagon
parked under the trees at the curb,
with a few children there at its window,
a single bulb under its roof, the light
spilling over my father's cousin, Ronald,
in his spotted white apron and cap
as he trickles a ribbon of butter
into the lined-up ten-cent popcorn bags.

Then think your way back up the streets
into the shadows, the Sousa marches
still pumping away but fading a little
with each house you pass. In the shadows
under the spreading porch roofs, old couples
sit on their creaky, pinging swings,
watching from silence the others, like you,
who left the park early, carrying children.

Imagine the warm weight of this child
as you carry him pressed to your breast,
for I am that child at this moment
and you are my father, carrying me
up dark Duff Avenue to the two-bedroom
house you recently borrowed to buy,
three blocks from the park, from the band's
last arrangement, a violet finale.

What you are feeling isn't legerdemain,
a phantom child in your arms, but a moment
I'm forcing upon you. You are already
beginning to smell things, leaves cooling
in the maples above, freshly mown grass.
And to hear things, somebody pushing a mower
long after dark in the light from a window,
not lifting his eyes as the two of you pass.

And, in an instant, I am too heavy to carry
and I walk at your side for a little while
but soon skip out ahead, and look back, and you
step up your pace but can never catch up,
and, in an instant, I am irretrievably
and altogether gone, the sound of my shoes
pattering over the sidewalk, then fading.
Maybe one day I'll come back, in a poem.

Behind you the band-shell park is emptying
and Dick Day is rolling his wooden band box
into a closet between ribs in the shell, locking
the door, and someone always out of sight
behind the arcs of color is waiting to switch off
what's left of the lights, and you sit alone
on your porch, moving your feet just enough
to swing an inch into the future and back.

II

Recital

The garbage truck's tires had left two keyboards
impressed in the snow, with the shadows of treads
for the sharps and flats, at least a hundred octaves
reaching far into a silence, and a tattered leaf
appeared as if out of thin air, sat down, and started
playing, first picking out a few simple scales, then
in a gust of breeze and confidence launched into
a complicated study composed for one hand,
too difficult, I would have thought, to be played
in front of songbirds, for there were cardinals,
finches, and juncos perched in the nearby bushes,
but on it played, and after a while as the wind
came up and swelled around us, the leaves above
burst into spontaneous applause, some of them
standing, and the birds nodded, one to another,
and the leaf that had played got up and stiffly
turned toward me and bowed, then bowed again,
and I began to clap along with all the others.

For a Friend, Ten Years Dead

Your outer door? With the cracked, milky plastic
tacked over the screen? It was hard to see through
when I stopped by and knocked, as if your little
glassed-in porch were filled with blowing snow,
a winter outside and a winter within, the door
hooked from the inside. Were you at home behind
that other, inner door, a dish-towel curtain
slack as a shroud in back of the icy glass?

Leaning against the wall by that inner door
was your broom, your tired red-handled one,
the straw bowed over to one side from ages
of cleaning-up-after, and on the black boot-mat
was the pie pan for your cat, and it was empty.

House Moving

With the earth between this house and the road
too muddy from snow, the movers have
driven away to wait out the winter
in a warmer place, leaving the house four feet
in the air on two steel I-beams, and the beams
on interlocking wooden blocks. And the wind,
with something new to do, is scouring out
the damp rock cellar, whistling a little,
wiping a hundred years of tattered cobwebs
from joists that haven't seen the light of day
since, as sweet-sour yellow two-by-tens,
they were hauled here and stacked in the grass.
If one of us had the guts to crawl in under
that cold blue shadow, pressing its four supports
into the sucking earth, I think we'd find
a breath of what was new here once, and fragrant,
still up there on the bottom side of time.

Ohio Blue Tip

I liked to watch him light his pipe
with a stick match pinched from the trough
of the matchbox holder nailed by the door
to the world, and how he popped it
to flame with the edge of his clamshell
thumbnail, and then how he drew
the fire down out of sight in the bowl,
then turned it loose, then did it again,
a cat-and-mouse game he was playing
with flame, and, though the fire tried
to cling to the match tip, how he flicked it
away with a snap of his wrist, though it
took two flicks to do it, and then how
the two of us studied the thin curl
of smoke as it lifted away from the tip
and then vanished, and it seemed he could
read something special in that, but he
never would say what it was.

An Overnight Snow

Before walking to work, and in still-falling snow,
my father in hat, suit, topcoat, and galoshes
would scoop our sidewalk. Only a few sounds
came in to me out of the predawn darkness:
the scrapes of not one but two shovels, each scrape
with a tap at the end to knock off the snow, then
a word or two, muffled, back and forth between
my father and our next-door neighbor, Elmo Mallo,
who was out shoveling, too. And later, after both
had gone to work and I'd be setting out for school,
I'd see their boot prints—can see them still, after
seventy years—my father's on one side of the line
where their shovels met, and Mr. Mallo's on the other.

Mother and Child

It was scarcely a park,
one corner of a block
scraped clean of whatever
had stood there, now seeded
and graveled, pinned down
by a half-dozen saplings.
At the center was one
of those red, blue, and yellow
plastic play sets, with a tube
to slide down. It was cold,
no one there but a woman
and child, wearing mufflers
and down-filled jackets
with hoods pursed in around
their faces, she standing
apart, patient, watching him
climb the blue blocky steps,
knee over knee, and then
the boy calling out with
a white puff of farewell,
vanishing into the mouth
of the big yellow tube
to appear at the bottom
again and again and again
as if to underline
something. What was it?
The woman, her hands stuffed
in her pockets, chin down
in her muffler, taking sips
of the air, the boy tasting
his lip with his tongue
as he climbed the blue steps,
and I only happening past.

Helping

Our basement floor sloped to the linty lid
of a drain, with a muddy-smelling darkness
through the holes, and when my mother's
wringer washer was left alone, its belly
sloshing and gurgling, digesting my father's
white shirts in a bath of bluing, it could be
counted on to sashay toward the drain
hoping to get a sniff, but at the last its leash
would restrain it, stretched tight to the outlet,
that washer too old to muster the strength
to yank the plug out of the wall, the furnace
looking on with amusement, its gray hair
rolled in enormous curlers as if it were
getting prepared to go away somewhere
although I knew it was far too fat to move.

There were washtubs, too, a pair of them
fastened together, like drums with the tops
peeled off, on metal legs with rubber casters
that shrieked when I'd try to push them
over the floor, and of course there were stairs,
thick planks with coats of gray enamel
down which my mother's boxy shoes came,
both shoes on each step, then her slightly
swollen ankles, and then the rickrack hem
of her apron, and then the rest of her,
slowly, a step at a time to keep from falling,
her arms around a load of what our lives
kept getting dirty and were wearing out,
those days when I was three or four or five
and waiting in our basement, helping.

At Dusk, in December

Driving a gravel road in the country
I saw a hawk fly up out of a ditch
with a mouse in its beak, and it flew
along beside my car for a minute,
the mouse still alive, its little legs
running as fast as they could, and there
we were, the three of us, all going
in the same direction, west, at just
a little under forty miles per hour.

Bread

I saw a man coming out of a day-old baked goods store
with two white plastic bags of something, held out like
the pans on the jeweler's scale that he was becoming
as he turned and walked away, presenting his back
and the outstretched beams of his arms with their bags
of bread or pastries suspended, an overlarge man
who rocked on the fulcrum of his dainty feet, the bags
rocking, too, the one on his right side lifting a little
when his weight settled onto his left foot, and vice versa.
Whatever was in those bags, or on that scale, he was
clearly a man on balance with himself, who knew exactly
how much of his life he was weighing and what it had cost
as, with an extra tip of the fulcrum, swinging his bags,
he rocked around the corner drugstore and was gone.

Winter Deaths

That snowy February the deaths came at us
from far offshore, three in one week, and though
the death ship lay at anchor below the horizon,

it seemed to know within only a few yards
where we mourners were standing, at graveside,
and it was triangulating fire. Each shelling

shook us right to our knees, throwing up snow
and chunks of wet, black sod, the craters so close
we could smell the miles lying beneath us,

not only the odors of clay, mold, and gumbo
but, strangely, of seawater, too, as if it were
welling up through those eons of limestone,

like time itself. Then the deaths stopped. A week
slowly passed, then another, and those of us
who'd survived stood softly talking together

through the now-lengthening days, our backs
to the graves as they healed, peering into
one another's stunned faces, then turning away.

At the Salvation Army Store

The man at the counter had a black brace
on one thumb and was loudly instructing
a young volunteer as to the best way
to display pairs of shoes in the window,
and the boy stood there patiently waiting
with a shoe in each hand, their toes too blunt
to point but pointing anyway, right toward
the man at the counter, as if they might
at any moment go galloping forward
and stomp him right into the floor. As I
browsed through the aisles I could hear
almost all of his monologue, the man's
voice raised as if to be certain I'd be
able to hear him, all the way back to
the book rack, then over in knickknacks,
words shoving their way through the aisles,
jostling the bony old shoulders of shirts,
brushing the white but now yellowing blouses
with their lily-of-the-valley fragrance.
It was a voice that would sink its fangs
into your ankle and never let go. I found
a novel I wanted, and walked to the counter
and paid, and the man at the register
punched in the keys without using his thumb,
his voice a little softer now that I'd come
within closer range, but still yammering on
at the young volunteer, who stood waiting,
holding one sorry old shoe in each hand.

Another World

It was one of those common goldfish bowls
in the shape of a mantel clock, curved sides
and a flat face front and back, two fish
with tails that swept along behind them
for the clock's two hands, though they were
loose and swam through time, ahead and back,
with nothing to age or change, just hours
of kissing the lips of their own reflections
and swimming past the tilted plastic anchor
as each delivered a bubble, always the same
tiny bubble, bright as a bead of mercury,
up to the locked door of the aqua castle.
Oh, now and then a sprinkle of fish food
momentarily clouded the mirror above,
then, zigzag, drifted down, and the fish would
swirl as if dancing in veils to catch the flakes
as they fell. But that was all that happened,
ever. All was well. But when I awoke
from dreaming in that easy, timeless world
I had to leave the timeless part behind.

After a Heavy Snow

I watched, from my window, a thin man
of indeterminate age—for only part
of his face, in dark glasses, was revealed
by the hood of his jacket—watched him
kick past my house in shoes so encrusted
with snow that all I could see of them
was that they weren't suited for winter,
with low tops, and what appeared to be
bare ankles or soaked white stockings,
yet he kicked at the snow as if with great
pleasure, big rooster tails flying ahead,
while behind him he pulled the short sled
of his shadow, and he kicked his way past
and was gone. And then, a little later,
I watched him come back, though this time
with his shadow in front, as he nudged it
along with the toe of one foot, as I'd once
done myself, pushing a sled out ahead,
both of those legs probably numb now
and raw as a rash at the ankles, and he
came and he went, and I leaned out to watch
him kick past, all the way to the corner.

A Letter from Never Before

It arrived with the rest of the mail
in our box by the road, came
bearing a standard Forever stamp,

a little American flag, and the letter
handwritten in pencil. "You don't
know me," it opened. "Never before

have I written to you. . . ." It had a quaint
syntax, its rhythm like that of
a waltz that was ever so gracefully

taking me into its arms. It had no
past to offer, only the present, as if
everything started from there,

with that Never Before, and this
on such an ordinary day, a few clouds,
birds flying high in the clouds,

then this, a few words of thanks,
carefully chosen and shaped
with a No. 2 pencil, which I knew

had been recently sharpened,
all this from a stranger, setting out
for Forever from Never Before.

Dropped Ceiling

The grave has been left in the hands of two men
with a backhoe, and already the funeral lunch
has been eaten, the mourners have driven away
from the Legion Hall, and it happened so fast,
first the death, then the mourning, then goodbyes
and goodbyes and goodbyes, the foam plates
packed in black bags by the door, the thermostat
next to the kitchen already turned down, tables
cocked out of place, the folding chairs in disarray,
the floor messed by galoshes that dripped snow
from the churchyard—work for the janitor later,
all of it *ashes to ashes*—the only available light
through a small front window displaying a curb
heaped with snow. Between us and the next world
is a fiberboard ceiling like so many thousands
of others, two-by-two tiles in a frail metal grid,
sagging in spots as if cupping the great weight
of the dust, rust, and air in the stale space
above it, where a patterned stamped-tin ceiling
coated with ancient enamel makes a fit roof
above that temporary stop for a departing spirit,
while below the dropped ceiling, dust sifts down
through the pores in the tiles, like time. We see it
on the coatrack's hangers waiting to be chimed.

III

Spring Landscape

A wake of black waves foamy with pebbles
follows the plow, rolls all the way up
to the fence, slaps into the grass and trickles
back, while farther out a spray of white gulls,
wings like splashes, are splashing down.
Spring on the prairie, a sky reaching forever
in every direction, and here at my feet,
distilled from all that blue, a single drop
caught in the spoon of a leaf, a robin's egg.

Man at a Bulletin Board

He is just one of the many we pass without seeing.
Today he's standing in out of the rain at the puddled
entrance to the supermarket, a few feet back from
the automatic doors which, gliding open at so little
as a sparrow's shadow, admit a chill that makes
the notices flutter: lost dogs and cats, announcements
on Easter-egg-colored paper, the newest tacked on top
of the out-of-date, the already-sold. He's head-to-toe
in grays, with wet shoes we notice with cast-down eyes
in walking past, which with those of other customers
have muddied the vinyl before crossing the inner
threshold into the store's colossal fluorescence,
into the faint kerosene odor of carrots, the shuffle
and snap of paper bags at the checkouts. His arms
are empty, slack at his sides. He might be on his way
in to buy something or out without buying, or
has he appeared here to let it all wash over him:
the harried young woman with a child in her cart
kicking the Pampers, two hard men side by side
with identical twelve-packs, and an elderly woman
with two bananas, awaiting the Senior Handi-Van?
He's almost invisible, this angel on watch, standing
a little apart, now reaching out and with one finger
pressing the corner of one of the fluttering bulletins
with studied interest, pretending to read as we pass.

At Dawn

I watched
a junco
climb a spruce
as if upon
a spiral stair
as branch to
branch it hopped
up round
and round
through green
not lifting wing
to touch
the banisters,
gray bird
with pearly breast,
all purpose,
who had soon
achieved the topmost
bobbing step
and, as if it
thought of it
the whole way up,
hopped off
upon the sky
and flew away.

In April

The roadside ditches are running ankle-deep
in green, where spring has spilled a gallon
of April, and it seems as if the wild plum bushes
have accidentally brushed against the clouds
and are tipped with a white that looks as fresh
as blossoms, though in a week they'll all be brown,
for it's impossible to keep the dust away
from any color painted on Nebraska, despite
the thin, transparent drop cloths of the rains.

A Floating Bottle

River within it, river without,
it bobs downstream, its long neck
catching the sun. It carries a cup
of muddy water from somewhere
upriver, and shoulders its way
through the light like a woman
with an apron-load of dirty onions,
or like a drunk, pitching forward,
about to be sick. Before the mind
can take it in (in every way it is
or might be), it is gone, one glint
among the many, far away.

Buttons

On a slick clay slope the Mississippi
licked at night and day, the button factory
stood with one floor at the edge of the water
and two above, fronting on Front Street
in Guttenberg, Iowa. Built of stone blocks
cut from the high yellow bluffs that rose
back from the river, it had once been
a busy place, making buttons for shirts,
for collars, pearl buttons of all sizes,
but had been closed up and shuttered
for decades. It was lofty and drafty,
the glass gone from the high windows,
the floors creaky and splattered with lime
from the pigeons. When I was a boy
there were scatters of mussel shells
down the slope to the edge of the water,
tumbled shine over shine over shine,
the light trickling down into the open
pink saucers of some, or over the rippled
black backs of the others, most of them
bored with three pearly holes. Holding
a shell up, you could see three vignettes
of the river at once: the one on the left
through which the languid brown water
was entering, easing downstream; the hole
in the middle showing the flow moving
faster as it passed by the spot on the bank
where I stood looking on; and, through
the one on the right, I could see where
the river was going, passing into the glare
of the midsummer morning, gone like
the buttons, thousands of new buttons,
coat buttons, shirt buttons, shoe buttons
sixteen for a dime, not one left behind.

A Caesura

He has been walking along among others
when his steps start to lag, and he stops,
and the others sidestep out and around
as he stands there, a snag in a river, bent
a bit forward, his ordinary human head
shining a little, with no hat and thin hair,
his eyes halfway closed, his ordinary hands
first clenching, then opening again, as if
to a pulse, the others not seeming to notice.

And then, quite suddenly, he awakens
from wherever he went in that moment,
from whatever he'd stopped to peer into,
and opens his eyes onto the brightness
that's all over everything and everyone
passing around him, and he steps ahead
into the stream, not ever quite to catch up
with the others, but swinging his arms
a little more than he needs to, striding
away from whatever has happened.

A Portrait Photograph

L.S. 1941–2017

Today you've returned, a lifelike figurine
in a midnight-black dress, nudged into light
by an invisible finger, a drapery
of brown shadow closing behind you.

Somebody's back there, peeking through
folds of death to see how we'll respond to
what's been placed before us after two
or can it be nearly three years gone?

The likeness is good but not quite perfect,
hair in a chignon, not fragrant and blowing,
and the smile was applied by someone
who didn't know how you warmed to kisses

when all of us were young. On the breast,
as if to call attention to itself, is a locket
bright as a star, as if we are to understand
that who you really were is closed forever.

Rain after Dark

The barns, in clear plastic slickers of rain,
stand at the side of the muddy gravel road
where they wait for the men to come home
from the tavern in a fleet of old pickups
awash in the misty gray waves of the hills,
the beds heavy with ballast: steel fence posts,
spools of wire, log chains, a grain scoop
for paddling, a five-gallon bucket for bailing,
and tanks of resentments recently topped,
the caps loose and reeking with fumes.

A Woman and Two Men

I was past in an instant. It was raining,
just softly, after a morning-long shower,
no sounds but the hiss of the pavement,
my wipers whupping on low. Two men
in hardhats were parked on the shoulder
in a truck with a ladder rack and a bed
full of tools. A woman driving a pickup
with a camper had pulled up a few yards
behind them and had walked up the road
to the passenger's side, her hair wet,
her arms wrapped about her. She had
boots, a fringed leather jacket with beads
on the fringe, and jeans with galaxies
of rhinestones on the pockets. The man
on the passenger's side had rolled down
his window, but only partway, and was
staring out over the hood while the driver
leaned far forward and over to talk,
his shoulder pressed into the wheel,
all this in a flash, those three at the side
of the highway, the fourth glancing over
in passing. I could in that instant feel
something common between us, among us,
around us, within us. It was more than
a light April rain playing over a road.

Vulture

I watched a vulture fly into a gusty wind,
tipping its wings one way and then the other,
just as a tightwire walker might hold out
a pole as he made his way over the world,
like Philippe Petit, who crossed the windy space
(his pole like wings, bending and rocking)
between the towers of the World Trade Center,
which today are space as well. The vulture
was bending its neck just a little, to peer
down into death, there far below.

Training to Be Blind

They are not yet blind, but are learning
to feel their way into a darkness
that slowly bleeds in from the edges.

They practice in pairs, walking the streets
in black blindfolds, each tapping a cane
the way a moth taps with a foreleg,

feeling the light. They talk, but do not
turn to each other because they are
looking ahead, seeing what can't be seen

coming. It's a halting conversation,
made around obstacles, their voices
slowly picking up each word and then

carefully setting it down, their free hands
lifting and settling like birds
at the cold edge of a sea. For this day,

they have chosen their clothes
for color, for style, but a time will come
when everything to touch their skins

will be merely weather. Two by two
they come toward us through traffic,
helping each other move into the future.

Tarnish

Unrolled from a sleeve of green felt
after years in a chest in the attic,
the family silverware has gone ghostly
with inky fingerprints of tarnish,
which for years have been feeling
their way forward through time
in the manner that flat black paint
on the back of a mirror picks its way
through to the front, as if wanting to
take part in whatever's reflected,
in this instance a very old woman
bent alone at her table, peering down
into the past in the bowl of a spoon.

Farmyard Light

for Don Williams

This one's been fixed to the top of a pole
poked into the center of everything,
and it looks like a stick with a puff of
yellow cotton-candy light spun round it
through which a few bats flit so expertly
that none of the light gets stuck to their
hunger. The barn and grain bins, though,
have got it all over their homely faces
and a single strand drapes from the pole
to the house. Out at the edge of all this,
a deaf old shed leans in, turning the ear
of a broken window as if trying to hear
the music of the carousel upon which
a frightened moth rides round and round.

Starling

From a fourth-story hotel window
looking out into rain, I watched
a starling make its way across
the low-sloping ribbed-metal roof
of a nearby building, hopping up
on each rib, then jumping down,
walking the spaces between them,
apparently intent on making it
on foot all the way over the roof
to its end, maybe seventy feet,
a distance any bird could cover
in an instant, flying. But no, this
starling was walking, although
the roofing was shiny with rain
and must have been slippery.
I expected that at any moment
it might give up and fly away,
but on it hopped as if it were
unaware that someone might be
high up in a window watching.
And though I couldn't hear it,
I supposed it was talking to itself
in the manner of starlings, and
enjoying the shine on its feet—
hop, step, and hop—the roof
all the more vast for its efforts,
with me its witness, the two of us
joined by the rain to a bit of forever.

Cover the Earth

The world hung high on the side of a shed
at the lumberyard, a plywood disk painted green,
with a small but apparently bottomless bucket
of red enamel tipped and pouring over it, the red
running down over all of America, dripping away
from its sides, and as we leaned our bicycles into
the turn up Northwestern Avenue toward the park
with its two miserable bears in their stinky cages,
in big blocky letters it told us to COVER THE EARTH
and we've done just that, and though those bears
died long ago, and though that sign was taken down
so many years ago that few remember it, just now
I leaned into another turn and saw it there.

IV

A Town Somewhere

I'd like to find it for you but I can't. You might not
like it anyway. It's quaint and pretty in an old
worn way, quite near to me at times. But then it's
gone, impossible to find. I've been there always
but I haven't been, if you can understand. It's a town
that I remember in sweet detail that was never.

It would be simple to find someone to love,
it's so open there. Wherever there's a fence around
a stand of flowers—bachelor's buttons—there's a gate
with a hook-and-eye latch that a finger can lift,
and wherever you see shutters framing windows,
they're decorations only, for they shut out nothing.

Those windows are Windex clean, too, sprayed
and wiped with wads of inessential news.
If you peer deep into the liquid shadows, careful
to avoid stirring the surface, you might see a figure
rising, as if to take a breath of what's beyond,
looking out at you above a sill of potted violets.

Was she the person you might love? She's gone.
And even as I call up the town for you I feel it
darken. Sundown. A dog is in the distance barking
and barking, as if aware that we'd been there
just passing through, leaving no more than a scent
on the wind where no one was, or seemed to be.

Raspberry Patch

Summer is in and under and around each leaf
and thorny cane and every weed and stalk of foxtail
woven among them, as if this were a tank brim-full
of green, a slosh of sun-warmed greens without room
for a breath between one leaf and the next but for
a few white bindweed flowers bubbling into the light
and buoys of berries bobbing on the surface,

where during the night a black-and-yellow spider
has spun an elaborate web, putting a dusty shine
on one soft wash of green, and now, astraddle
its center, pulls it together, one thin leg flexed
on every spoke, shaking the dewdrops free, closing
the hole beneath her feet through which a little
light has trickled, fallen, and been lost forever.

There's butterfly milkweed, too, its flowers dipped
in a kettle of fire, with white and blue butterflies
coming and going, staggering, finding their way
through the hot July air, stumbling along over
boulders of light, then clawing up onto the rough
sponge-like tops of the blossoms, and stepping out
onto them, kneeling to sip at the freshets of orange.

Then poison ivy as well, with waxy leaves of three,
more bindweed with those tiny morning-glory flowers,
and sticky vines of wild cucumber, all of which
have over many summers learned how best to climb
the thorny berry stalks without hurting themselves,
and closer to the earth, a twiny length of creeper
has crept unseen from miles away and years before.

And behind the patch, where the plywood siding
of the old garage lifts a yellow cuff and steps
over its own cool stone foundation, is a damp
black burrow leading down and in and under,
a slide of mud dug slightly larger with each spring,
where a groundhog lolls in semidarkness, and can hear
from time to time a berry drop and roll a little way.

Sounds of a Summer Night

Up to his smile in the pond,
the leopard frog plays his kazoo.

A June bug plunks the dobro
of a window screen.

On a leaf, the tree frog strokes
her washboard with a twig.

A bobwhite toots two notes
on a pennywhistle.

Bellied in mud, a bullfrog
blows down the neck of a jug.

Owl on the ocarina,
raccoon on the trashcan,

but not a sound from the snake
who slips through the night

in his tight black leather suit,
guitar picks sewn all over it.

Noon Whistle

The siren on the village water tower
is each noon wound onto the spool of itself,
then released, and the sharp end
springs out and slaps at the fading barns
and pig sheds all over the township,
blisters the sides of big square farmhouses,
then reaches out over the partly turned fields
to wake the old farmers, wheeled up
to their nursing home windows or dead,
nagging at them to leave their teams
and four-bottom plows, letting the horses
cool off, hanging their heads, reins
drooling down, and to limp in over
the fresh black clods toward chicken,
new potatoes, and green beans for lunch
in the silence that rushes back in.

Vespers

The streetlamps come on, one by one,
as darkness washes in, and soon

there is only a cone-shaped buoy of light
afloat at the end of each block, clanging

with color, its surface glittering
with moths, something to steer by.

A Broken Sidewalk

In a town in Iowa where I had stopped
to stretch my legs, I found an old sidewalk
buckled by roots where great white maples
had wedged fingers in under the slabs,
trying, I supposed, to reach the damp gutters
at the edge of the street. And there they'd been
caught by the knuckles, as though under
the sash of a great glass pane through which
the people who lived along that street
peered out at the world. Above me, the trees
rested their foreheads against the cool glass
as if they'd surrendered, and there I was,
adding my weight, though I felt as light
as a spider, stepping along the chipped top
of that sash, over the broken gray caulking.

A Place under a Roof

A summer ago, a little brown bat
slept through the days tucked into a corner
up under our roof, and coming and going,

I'd look up to see it there, like a wallet
or coin purse that someone had tried to hide,
hooking it over a nail, not much within it

but sleep. Every night the whole sky
belonged to the bat, but each day it had
just this one spot, and that corner

became ours, the bat's place in the shadows
and my place to peer into, finding it there.
This summer it's gone. There's a wasp nest

the size of a golf ball just inches away
that's alive with black wasps, but a nest
doesn't fly off each night and flutter

back in the morning. Yet there's a place
in that corner which, only for me now,
is ours, still full of both of us, empty.

The Dead Vole

In blinding sunlight on my open hand,
it was no longer than the first two joints
of my little finger, its eyes so small
I couldn't see them for the fur, its tail
no longer than a stem, no, half the length
of the stem on, what, a cherry, or, better,
that of a grape, for it was dark as a grape,
the rest of its tail probably still on a vine
in the clouds that it dropped from, this
dab of thunderhead gray, too light to make
even as much sound as a raindrop, and
with a dry speck of a nose that might
have been sniffing my palm, for it
appeared to be that much alive, although
it weighed nothing, a leaf on the wind,
as if it could catch at not only a breeze
but no more than a breath and fly off,
but even such a minuscule being, I thought,
ought to weigh something in death,
a little more than itself, even if only to
hold it down under, though not nearly
as heavy as the few things you'd find
on a walk up your lane to the road,
like a bolt fallen out of an oil pan,
or a skeleton key or a nickel, but
at least as much weight as a grape or
the pit of a cherry spat out at the edge
of the gravel leading back to your house,
with no mail today in the box by the road,
and the small, indescribable weight
of no weight to the death in your hand.

Apron

Most of the time it hung flat
down her flat front, like a shade
drawn over a window. No one

could see within her, or who
she really was, all grays behind it,
her legs below it, thin in loose

brown stockings coarse as burlap,
fallen in rings above her slippers,
their insteps slit for comfort.

Some afternoons in apple time
she'd be out in her yard, the hem
bunched up in one hand, forming

a basket, while with the other
she'd pick out only three or four
nice apples, leaving a hundred

hanging. Passing by, you wouldn't
have noticed her inside the arms
of that tree, a cobbler's worth

of apples clutched in her apron,
invisible woman, tilted a little
to favor the leg on the right.

A Heron

Maybe twenty yards out from the shoreline
a great blue heron waited, motionless,
upon a post that seemed to have no purpose
other than to stand there stained with rings
of history as the old lake, breathing sunlight,
rose and fell.

The heron was the color of the water
so that it seemed that I could see the water
through her, as if she were a creature blown
of glass, not smeared by anybody's fingers,
still clean and delicate and waiting to be filled
with color

although I saw that she was filled already,
from the bulb of her body to the tip of her beak,
not with a color that anyone knew but with
a cloudy fluid that had been distilled
from summer light and now was being aged
and mellowed

though how much longer it might take was
anybody's guess. But I had been imagining
too long, and she had felt it, too, that threat
of too much beauty being forced upon her,
and spread her glassy wings and lifted off
and flapped away across the water.

A Shadow

for Jared Carter

Dust whispered to the shadow under the bridge
and told it whose team and wagon were crossing
and how it could know whose it was by the clop

of the hooves—each team had its own rhythm—
and by the distinctive tock-tick of the wheels
as they knocked over the planks. The shadow

made notes on the long scroll of the water
using the tip of a willow branch, but the notes
disappeared under its eyes as if written in

vanishing ink. Counting the farm wagons
that crossed just one old one-lane bridge in one
little township could prove to be boring,

but if you'd been born to a long line of shadows—
bridge after bridge after bridge all the way out
to the hazy horizon—counting the wagons

and horses was what was expected of you.
And while the men and their teams were all day
in the sun, riding those clattering wagons

empty out onto the fields, then back, loaded
with hay—the wheels' sound by then always
different, hammering down through the timbers—

the work of the shadow took place in shade
and was mostly just counting and listening,
cooling its feet in the water that trickled

down out of time, cutting a shadowy track
like a cow path, carrying clouds and sometimes
a few homely pigeons with news from afar.

Up the Block

Maybe you saw me pass by, walking,
or maybe you didn't. I raised a hand
in a tentative wave, but you were intent
upon your watering, as if to make sure
the spray from the hose fell evenly
over your small plot of petunias, purple,
pink, and white. The nozzle was yellow,
of plastic, much like a showerhead,
sweeping or brushing the bright drops
evenly, lacquering over the flowers,
the dark purple ones deeper in color
under the layers of glazes, and the pink
brighter, too. The white looked the same,
but you'd probably planted those there
mostly to set off the others. From one end
to the other you slowly and gently
swept the soft whiskbroom of droplets,
enrapt, or so it appeared, by what
you saw sprinkling out of your hand,
upon which I could see drops forming,
each diamond-bright on a knuckle,
and I'd guess they were cold, perhaps
even numbing, but you'd gotten hold
of a rainbow, and couldn't let go.

Rabbit Hutches

to the memory of William Stafford

You'll find them sometimes in those small towns
pushed off to the side by a four-lane bypass
that avoids the boarded-up motels and shut-down
filling stations bald in the trees at the junky edge,
those highways gaining a little distance, too,
from whatever's reaching up and out and over—
the steeples, Catholic and Lutheran, the tin-clad
co-op elevator, the water tower with the town's name
turned to the side. Somewhere within a place
like that, propped up on rotting two-by-fours,
you'll find a little row of rabbit hutches, three
or four, their doors thrown open, shingles gone,
the plywood floors sour and delaminating,
wire netting torn and rusty, all that's left
of someone's good idea gone bad and left behind,
poor peach-crate hutches hammered up against
whatever might be slightly stronger for a while
until there's not much standing but a steady wind,
whining with semis passing on the four-lane,
stirring a little tuft of soft white rabbit fur.

Tree Frog

Late evening, a velvety black
beyond the high windows, and on one
a tiny tree frog with its legs spread
presses its soft, white belly to the glass.
This night it gets to be the evening star.

Farm Wagon

I pull out the four chunks of moldy old firewood,
one from under each wheel, and the wagon, heavy
when empty, when given a shoulder to rock the wheels
out of their dents in the earth, slowly starts to roll
down the slope of this poem, through a pasture,
its wheels with their tight iron bands striking sparks
from a few of the words it rolls over and knocks
to the side. I am running alongside it as, faster and
faster, it careens down the hill toward the high bank
of the creek, bordered by springy young willows
that a wagon like this one can shove through without
trying. Some of these words, like dry leaves on the floor
of the box, are trying to leap out but fall back. It's all
moving quickly, but I want you to see what I see
before it rolls over the edge: the tongue's out in front,
tapping the slope like the cane of a blind man,
a blind man in a hurry, and one side of the box
has been built up a couple of feet higher, the planks
loose in the frame, rattling now, but when your
great-grandpa was handpicking corn it would sound
only once when each ear rapped this bang-board,
and his good horse, old Dolly, knew from that sound
to take a step forward, on to the next stalks of corn,
very slow work, handpicking a whole field, but
now you might say I've unharnessed the past,
and it may well leap out from the willowy bank,
out over this second-to-last line with its dry creek
below, and, with luck, rattle on into forever.

Red Stilts

Seventy years ago I made a pair of stilts
from six-foot two-by-twos, with blocks
to stand on nailed a foot from the bottom.

If I was to learn to walk on stilts I wanted
them red and I had to wait almost forever
for the paint to dry, laid over the arms

of a saggy, ancient Adirondack chair
no longer good for much but holding hoes
and rakes and stakes rolled up in twine,

and at last I couldn't wait a minute longer
and took the stilts into my hands and stepped
between them, stepped up and stepped out,

tilted far forward, clopping fast and away
down the walk, a foot above my neighborhood,
the summer in my hair, my new red stilts

stuck to my fingers, not knowing how far
I'd be able to get, and now, in what seems
just a few yards down the block, I'm there.

V

In Early August

At dusk I glanced out one of our west windows
and saw a stirring in the golden air, the way
a glass of water stirs when some enormous truck
drives past, but this was dragonflies, a hundred
or more out hunting together, darting and diving,
snatching mosquitoes or gnats from the last light
of the afternoon. Each was its own, with its own
small part of the work to do, like men with sandbags
damming a rising tide, and what it was that they
were holding back, it seemed to me, was nightfall,
and they held it a long, long time as I looked on,
afraid to step outside and stand among them,
not knowing what there'd be that I could do.

The Couple

Under a sky of white fluorescence
and surrounded by chattering gulls,
the waves of her illness would lift them

then let them fall, and in each trough
they took on a little more water,
the test results spilling over the rails,

but both were still able to bail
and they bailed, she in the bow, looking
forward, and he in the stern, his eyes

on her back, her shoulders, the light
in her well-kept hair. Days passed,
weeks passed, months passed until

she'd lost the strength for bailing,
and all the color had been bleached
from his hopeful face, but still

they drifted on, a clamor of gulls
surrounding them, calling out
to one another, a dizzying flurry

of white that followed their boat
as now, riding low in the water,
it floated toward the gray horizon,

that ever-leveling line, and it seemed
he'd have to swim a long, long way
if he were ever willing to return.

A Roadside Cemetery

Some of the old stone markers had broken
away from their bases and fallen, some of them
broken in falling, and the long succession
of old men who cared for the graves—always
old men—had carried the pieces up into
the shade of two great, ancient Scots pines
and leaned them around the trunks, the way
a man might lean the scrap ends of boards
around something he wanted to burn. For years
those stones leaned there, and lichens grew gold
on those that leaned back from the sun
on the south, and moss had grown over the ones
in the shade to the north. It all felt balanced,
those stones held up by trees, trees holding stones.

From time to time I'd stop by to spend time
in what seemed very close to permanence,
and although the weather was always at work,
softening the names and dates into whispers,
I thought that this would last. Then one day
I found that the trees were gone, their stumps
gone too, ground out, damp dust in the grass.
The sun was everywhere, all over everything,
brighter and more merciless than it had ever
been before, a glare on every standing marker,
bleaching the little flags and plastic flowers.
I had to shade my eyes to find those stones
I felt were mine, stacked up like phone books
by the fence, with lichens burning like a field
of wheat on top of the topmost stone, arranged
in three pieces, the inscription turned down.

Autumn Equinox

I was driving straight into the rising sun
on a dusty country road when out of it
came a school bus, going too fast, I thought,
for driving on gravel, yellow light filling it
back to front, a soft halo around the head
of the driver. It was trailing a long cocoon
of glowing dust that it seemed to be trying
to free itself from, but the tips of its slick
yellow wings were stuck in the opening.
I had to pull over hard, far to the right,
to let it go past, my two right wheels
off in the weeds on the spongy shoulder,
and I glanced up at the flashing windows
and saw the silhouetted heads of children,
all facing forward, trusting the bus and
the driver, trusting in me to swerve out of
the way, trusting in everything, being
borne along at a frightening speed into
the dust that I'd lifted while driving a road
I'd felt was all mine, that had suddenly
gone dark in my car's mirror. A shadow
of something far out of reach of this road
had raced past, far beyond stopping.

Cleaning a Chimney

Cleaning a farmhouse chimney with a log chain
would make its own soft music—solo piano, the notes
mellowed by soot, and no one nearby to hear them
but the performer as he lowered his cold chain
though the octaves, his feet pressing the shingles
as if pressing the pedals, glancing up now and then
at the cloudy sheet music all along the horizon.

Sixtieth Reunion Banquet

From left to right they have begun
to pass the dream, a crystal platter
upon which each of them places
a piece of the past, and though it
should be growing heavier, it isn't,
having begun now to lift, as if to
float from hand to hand around
the table, no more than a breath
on the tips of their fingers,
and even when one of them takes
a moment suddenly remembered
and looks at it from every angle,
then stuffs it into her purse
for safekeeping, or into his wallet,
one of the others adds a memory
to keep it balanced, then passes
it on, and the dream grows ever
lighter, and brighter, too, as if lit
from within by colored fires,
and when at last it's gotten so full
that bits start to spill from its edges,
they nudge it to the table's center
and look upon it with delight
as it floats there, gently rocking,
inches above the invisible shadow.

A Moth, a Moon

I watched a moth fly round and round the moon,
or so it seemed as I stood looking up.

More than two hundred thousand miles away,
the moon was small, and full, and very bright

like a lightbulb over a neighbor's door.
The moth was the size of a moth, but next to

the faraway moon it looked big, like a satellite
orbiting, held in place by the moon like a moth

by the glow of a bulb, and it seemed to be
spanking the face of the moon with its wings

the way that a moth will spank a lightbulb.
The explanation, of course, was that the moth

had chosen to fly round an invisible spot
directly between where I stood and the moon. . .

Although maybe not, maybe the moon I could see
wasn't our everyday moon, far off in the stars,

but another, smaller one, and this little moon
was the size of a cabbage, magically floating

over my house, wrinkly and pale like a cabbage,
for the moth had a cabbage moth's whiteness,
and flew in and out of the light like a star.

Suitcase

You've seen others like it in the tan light
of an attic or perhaps in a closet
with musty black shadows on hangers.

Pull it into the light by a handle
of cracked leatherette, you can feel that it's
unaccustomed to hands, its two snaps

biting down on themselves. But now,
in the light, it's becoming a warm,
welcoming blue, like a late autumn sky

with a little brown dust from a harvest
mixed in. And how can you not open it
now, though you know that there's

nothing inside? Only the sound of snaps
snapping back on themselves with a rap
on that blue pasteboard soundboard

and the stained and torn lining, thin as
a nightgown, pink and blushing, exposed
all at once with its powdery fragrance.

Shame

You were a college student, a waitress
paying your way through the sixties,
and I was recently divorced, alone
and lonely, looking for someone to love
in those dreary years when it seemed
no one else was willing "to make
a commitment," as we said back then,
and I mustered my courage and asked you
to dinner, and met you at your door,
and we walked downtown, both of us shy,
both awkward, both scented and scrubbed
and overdressed and clopping along
in new and uncomfortable shoes,
and over wine and dinner, as we began
to feel more comfortable together,
sometimes touching each other's hands,
I told you my story and you told me
yours, the way young people will,
you finishing yours with the news
that you had leukemia, the slow kind
that with "adequate treatment"
could keep you alive, at least for a time,
and it frightened me, having no courage
for anyone's pain but my own, knowing
nothing at all about love, and surely
you must have been terribly hurt
to read all that in my expression,
and fifty years later I'm still ashamed
to have been the kind of person
who could then walk you back to your door
still early in the evening, and leave you
there with a dry little kiss and a promise,
who would never phone, who would avoid
the restaurant where I'd first seen you
wiping the tables, working your way

through so much more than college,
you in your starched uniform apron
with a plastic tag pinned to your breast
and your name that I've even forgotten.

Driving to Dwight

Before I could get to the place where I saw it,
that young fox was gone, having looked up
from whatever it had found on the road
and was playing with, cricket or field mouse.
It had seen my car coming and scampered off
into the long grass of the ditch. Four things
were gone in that instant: first, the fox;
then its playfulness, too, seeing its dancing
on the gravel, batting at whatever it found
with a paw; and third, whatever it found,
so small it too had disappeared; and last
was that featureless vent in the grass
that had opened for these, then had closed,
disappearing into its greens. The fifth thing
wasn't gone: my delight, to come upon
something like this for the very first time,
so far into my years—my car slowing down—
peering out into the world, hoping to
see it again. That joy hadn't scampered away
after the others. I caught it and carried it
this far, smoothing its fur, almost too happy
with having it happen to share it with you.

Battleship Gray

The tongue-and-groove floors of the open porches
on these old houses up in dry dock in the ports
of little towns have been painted again and again
always a coat of slightly tacky gray, the color
of what remained of Nimitz's Pacific fleet
in the years when in those shaded parlor windows
hung little flags with one star, gold or silver, for those
who served and, up under the pale blue ceilings—
always painted blue, a warm sky blue—were
slatted porch swings rigged high in their chains
for winter weather, like the last few lifeboats,
weak and leaky, only one small boat per ship.

Fairgrounds

A special kind of breathy stillness fills
an empty county fairgrounds on a late
October afternoon, and a cool, light-fingered,
pickpocket breeze runs in circles about you,
touching your buttoned-up jacket. Bleachers
upon which dozens of people were shelved
like jars of pickles and preserves are empty
but still warm to the touch, with sunlight
breaking through clouds that come and go,
waiting for something to start, perhaps
the first exhibition of snow, the earliest
and youngest snows first, led into the ring,
plumes lifted from the crowns of drifts.
But that is later; now it's just leaves, leaves
everywhere, up to the ankles, and in the bare
spaces among them, the rakes of the seasons
are smoothing the dust, erasing the footprints.
But I know you were here for the fair, and you
and you. I feel you all around me. And I, too,
was among you, living, and the last to leave.

On the Market

Their children came home, but not to stay,
to get the house ready to put on the market,
and they ripped up all the carpeting
because of the cats, and piled it on the curb
to be hauled away, beige, beige, and beige,
a mountain of stains soaked through
to the backing, but what they did with all
the cats is a mystery. They're gone today,
including the earless old tom I used to see
slinking back home in the morning,
not looking both ways before crossing,
and the parents, too, gone with the cats.

Deer Path

It's a track that wobbles a little as it crosses
the grassy slope, as if a wheelbarrow made it,
one heaped with wariness, though wariness
weighs almost nothing, is as light as a breath.
The deer walk east in single file at sunset, west
at dawn, testing each step with a tentative hoof
as if crossing a stream, their path just wide enough
for one, because they've never met another
coming back. By early morning they're at home
at the western edge of the pasture, out of sight
in the tangled sumac. All day they rest in polished
bowls of grass set out to catch those few warm
drops of deer, and when the sun is low, and casts
long shadows east, they each unfold and follow.

Woolly Caterpillar

I came upon you on a sidewalk,
black as a hyphen slowly crossing a page,
as if you were trying to connect
the last word in October with a word in
the April to come. From closer up
you looked like a casket being borne
by a half-dozen soldiers walking in step
and I stopped, as one would, as you passed.
Your casket was draped with the flag
of your country, orange like a leaf,
and there were clusters of old leaves,
many in orange, curled up in lawn chairs
all along the processional, younger ones
restless and darting about. I thought
I should take off my cap and I did,
and the late autumn wind in my ears
was the bugle that played, not so well,
as they carried you into the distance.

Applause

At the close of her solo recital
the young pianist bows, and her hair,
like a curtain of gold, falls over
her modesty, as if she were smiling
down into a pool, and as we stand

to applaud, she lifts up her face,
shining and bright from the kiss
of that mirroring water, then bows
once again. Our applause has the sound
of a sudden downpouring of leaves,

a warm yellow clatter like that of
a ginkgo in autumn, when it drops
every leaf, all at once, after a frost,
though this time the frost was those
crystalline notes that she shook

from the tips of her fingers. And now
she is shaking her head, as if to say
that all of this praise is too much,
but the clapping keeps leafing down,
even out of the balcony shadows.

About the Author

Red Stilts is Ted Kooser's fifteenth book of poetry in sixty years. He has also published five books of nonfiction, five children's picture books, and sixteen chapbooks and special editions. He served two terms, from 2004 to 2006, as the US Poet Laureate, and during his first term won the Pulitzer Prize for *Delights & Shadows* from Copper Canyon Press. He is the founder and editor of American Life in Poetry, a weekly column reaching 4.6 million readers in print and online. He lives with his wife, Kathleen Rutledge, in rural Nebraska, and teaches one class a year at the University of Nebraska–Lincoln—a tutorial in poetry writing for graduate students in the creative writing program. His most recent of many honors is the inauguration of the Ted Kooser Center for Medical Humanities at the University of Nebraska Omaha.

TO LEARN MORE ABOUT UNDERWRITING
COPPER CANYON PRESS TITLES,
PLEASE CALL 360-385-4925 EXT. 103

WE ARE GRATEFUL FOR THE MAJOR SUPPORT PROVIDED BY:

Lakeside Industries Inc. on behalf of Jeanne Marie Lee
Maureen Lee and Mark Busto
Peter Lewis and Johnna Turiano
Ellie Mathews and Carl Youngmann as The North Press
Larry Mawby and Lois Bahle
Hank and Liesel Meijer
Jack Nicholson
Gregg Orr
Petunia Charitable Fund and adviser Elizabeth Hebert
Gay Phinny
Suzanne Rapp and Mark Hamilton
Adam and Lynn Rauch
Emily and Dan Raymond
Jill and Bill Ruckelshaus
Cynthia Sears
Kim and Jeff Seely
Joan F. Woods
Barbara and Charles Wright
Caleb Young as C. Young Creative
The dedicated interns and faithful volunteers
of Copper Canyon Press

The Chinese character for poetry is made up of two parts:
"word" and "temple."
It also serves as pressmark for Copper Canyon Press.

The poems are set in Clarendon.
Book design and composition by Katy Homans.